Communication Beyond Words

Words

Connection Collection

GETTY AZOD

Editor: M.A. Bjarkman

Balboa Press books may be ordered through booksellers or by contacting:

Balboa Press
A Division of Hay House
1663 Liberty Drive
Bloomington, IN 47403
www.balboapress.com
1 (877) 407-4847

ISBN: 978-1-4525-9996-0 (sc)
ISBN: 978-1-4525-9997-7 (e)

Library of Congress Control Number: 2014922266

Print information available on the last page.

Balboa Press rev. date: 3/11/2015

BALBOA.
PRESS
A DIVISION OF HAY HOUSE

Communication Beyond Words

Connection Collection

Contents

Dedications

To my parents Abbas Ghajar Azodanloo and Azam Sarafi
I thank you for the strong foundation of Love and for teaching me to be a giver.

To my sister Felor Ghajar Rostami & my brother Alexander Azod
I thank you for being the instruments to raise me up to unconditional Love.

To my past Spiritual Teachers
I thank you for every word of wisdom and for new visions for my life.

To Drs. Ron and Mary Hulnick
I thank you for polishing my soul through the Consciousness, Health, and Healing Program.

Foreword

What is this human experience we call life really all about? There seems to be a mesmerizing, driving desire that keeps us yearning, asking, learning and reaching for something that we intuitively sense is gigantic and boundless and yet intensely intimate. Like life itself, the answers we seek mostly seem unclear, confusing, and at times distracting.

In both of our lives, we are in a space where neither of us could ever imagine it with our minds. Our perfectly planned life was gently or forcibly moved to a different direction and that road took us where we are today, where it's even more magnificent than we ever imagined it to be. Life really is what happens while we're making other plans. One thing that we both experienced, however, was amidst life's changing roads, whether it was because of Habib's cancer, or Sherry's journey of being the sole support for her family of 5 at the age of 19 yrs, we learned how to listen inwardly and outwardly and find our answers and directions, not in our heads but in our hearts.

We learned the harder we focus directly on our problems, the more the answers elude us. They remain invisible. During the dark times of our lives, we must learn to look away from the crisis at hand and focus on what surrounds it, the contributing factors and supporting situations. Then the answers will come into view, and we will see that our grievous situation has brought us a glorious gift that was just outside our field of vision. And All we need to take on this journey is vulnerability, authenticity, an open heart, and courage.

In *Communication Beyond Words*, Getty Azod provides similar illumination to the questions we all need answered in life. In turns intimate and enlightening, she invites us to join her along her life path as she experiences triumphs and challenges alike. With the kind of vulnerability that requires great strength, Getty opens her heart in these pages in service of providing universal experiences to which we all can relate. Her work here is a lesson for all of us in how to alter our perspective of a problem to find the answer, which is always hidden in plain sight. Communication with God is indeed without words and can come in subtle forms but with specific messages such as a uniquely-shaped rock that sits in our path, the smile from a stranger or the wording on a billboard that we happen to glance up at as we drive by. Spirit is speaking to us all the time providing the answers to our questions, but we must remain conscious and looking in the right places if the dialogue is to be sustained. Getty is the embodiment of communicating beyond words and is a master at capturing the symbolism of nature and interpreting the divine messages within it.

The philosophy of 13th century Persian poet and mystic, Rumi, is richly interwoven through the lush images and inspirational prose. We can say from experience that the words of Rumi resonate deeply with all those who consider themselves seekers, and the way Getty humbly offers herself to the spirit of his work is a testament for all of us to live the spiritual path of Rumi. This is why we call her a psycho-spiritual transducer, because she can grasp the ineffable messages of spirit and crystallize them in a way that is clear and comforting for all of us.

It was a blessing to read *Communication Beyond Words* and an honor to write the foreword to this second edition. It is our prayer that it touches your soul in a way that is deeply meaningful for you and that you recognize how the Divine has been speaking to you all along. Just remember that God never stops speaking. We stop listening. For those that have ears, let them hear and understand that God can speak through images and we can hear with our eyes. You can learn to communicate beyond words and that language is Love.

Dr. Habib Sadeghi & Dr. Shahrzad Sami
Los Angeles 2014

Endorsements

This is a book of spiritual romance bringing you into intimacy with your divine self.
It has a refreshing spirit that nourishes the dry lands of the soul, which allows the will's hidden
potentials to begin to appear. If you must love yourself, you can do it through this book.

This book woos you into loving yourself. This book invites you to see
yourself differently and to fall in love with yourself.

Brother Ishmael Tetteh
Founder/Director of Etherean Mission Int.
Author of Essential Life Education

Getty Azod's *Communication Beyond Words* is the equivalent of a divine pause,
of fully entering the present moment with a heart of ecstatic gratitude born of
the recognition that in every speck of space and measure of time we are
accompanied by an invisible, assisting Grace.

Michael Bernard Beckwith
Author of *Life Visioning*

Communication Beyond Words is a collection of spiritual truths. These truths as written in
Getty's, gentle, simplistic style, feel like a nature walk along the path of your soul. Her
stories are gentle reminders that nudge us deeper into the realization of how powerful
and deeply connected we are, to the Divine Source that connects us all as one
through nature.

Rev. Doreen Hamilton
Author of *Spiritually Speaking... Get Over It!*

Introduction

At one point of my life I truly wanted to know who I was and what my purpose in this life was. This wanting has taken me on a Journey of Spirituality for the past 20 years with many wonderful spiritual teachers and with a lot of my own dedication.

In 2013 I started the Consciousness, Health, and Healing (CHH) Program at the University of Santa Monica. Through this program I realized that we look for connection as a means of embracing Spirit. We come to understand how well we are supported by Divine Love. Moreover, through this awareness we are able to access an extraordinarily powerful conduit into the silent heart of our being.

Connection is one of the most profound techniques for cultivating an awakened consciousness and submerges us into the depths of its truth.

Cultivating both heartfelt questions and at the same time a willingness to open ourselves to receive Divine messages through signs, creates an expanded perception of life and offers us a glimpse into the mystery of Reality.

This book presents both statements of Universal Messages of Truth in answer to my heartfelt questions and a dynamic introduction to this connection and communication.

The stories in this book serve as an opening to access a greater dimension of ourselves and are a source of elevation to that dimension. Every page is a connection in the Universal Language of Beauty and Oneness.

I hope that after you read this book you will start writing in a stream of consciousness in your journal or notebook; whatever messages you find there are spoken from the sacred stillness of your being. I am here for you to answer any of your heartfelt questions. Go here to connect with me at www.daytodaybliss.com

May you experience the Communication Beyond Words often.

Acknowledgements

To M.A. Bjarkman, my editor, who was sent directly from Spirit
and who added a rich dimension to this body of work.

To my generous photographer and friend, Eric Weiss, for capturing
the essence of my true being in the pictures he took of me.

To Mr. Colman Barks, for giving me permission to use Rumi poems in my stories,
from book "Year with Rumi" . This book has been my Bible for the past 15 years.

To my family and staff, Alexander Azod, Abbas Ghajar Aazodanloo,
Termeh Joleh, and Dennis Ylo, for your unconditional support and
giving me the time and space to go through this life journey.

To Drs. Ron and Mary Hulnick, Dr. Lili Goodman-Freitas, Ms. Kristi Palma, and all the staff
at the University of Santa Monica, my love and appreciation for one year of service, and for
helping me nurture the seed of Consciousness, Health, and Healing, to become the source of
this book *Communication Beyond Words*.

The Journey

In 2013 I committed myself to a one year course in the Consciousness, Health, and Healing (CHH) program at the University of Santa Monica. Although, I had registered for this program and was committed to go through with it, I still had doubts. I was not sure if I could run my business, pay for tuition, attend classes and complete my homework with ease and grace. On the first day of school and before class started, I went to my meditation room, prayed and contemplated how to be with this program. In my stillness, my intention was to access the State of Consciousness that Rumi calls *"fana"* (which means "Nothingness and Poverty"). I asked Rumi to show me how to be with this program and what I should expect. I opened my Rumi book and the following poem was the message for that day.

This poem was the message I needed. The poem was talking about the state of being that was my desire to experience; however I never experienced it long enough to grasp the joy of it. This poem gave me courage and helped me to focus my attention on the task before me for the coming year. That was the true moment I committed myself to the CHH program, hoping to grasp the experience of *"fana"*.

Fire is whispering a secret in smoke's ear,

This aloeswood loves me

Because I help it live out its purpose.

With me it becomes fragrance,

And then disappears altogether.

The knots untie and open into absence,

As you do with me, my friend.

Eaten by flames, and smoked out into the sky,

This is most fortunate.

What's unlucky is not to change and disappear.

This way leads to humiliation and contempt.

We have tried the fullness of presence.

Now it's time for desolation.

Love is pulling us out by the ears to school.

Love wants us clean of resentment.

And those impulses that misguide our souls.

We are asleep, bur Khidr

Keeps sprinkling water on our faces.

Love will tell us the rest of what we need to know soon.

Then we'll be deeply asleep and profoundly awake

Simultaneously, like cave companions.

Connecting to The Power of Spirit

One autumn day some friends and I gathered in my back yard gazebo for a secret ritual. In our prayer we asked Spirit to guide us to center ourselves with Divine energy. Each one had to share about a situation that had disturbed them in the past few weeks and then ask for guidance from the others. I talked about my interaction with a friend whom I had upset. A week before our meeting this friend had come to my home and started talking disrespectfully about our teacher. I could not sit and listen to her and be part of this conversation. Also, I could not allow this kind of disrespect in my home. I asked her with a very firm voice, *"Do you think about the words coming out of your mouth before you say them? Why do you choose these words and talk this way? "* My questions upset her and she left my home with hard feelings. In the following week I kept asking Spirit if I had done the right thing and if I could have made my point in a kinder way.

As I started sharing this story in our secret ritual gathering, we suddenly saw a falcon fighting with other birds and then perching on the chair in the grassy area near us. As soon as we tried to take a picture, the falcon flew away. My home is in the middle of the city and I have never seen any falcons in this area. The falcon's job is to perch on the King's Hand and follow his instruction. I noticed that I was the falcon on the Hand of Spirit and I had shown my obedience to my King when I had asked my guest those questions. A week after our meeting I talked to that friend again and since that time we have established a deeper connection with more respect for each other and more harmony with our authentic selves. I became aware that I had used my power for the highest good of all.

The Beauty of Vulnerability

A few days ago I was walking with my dogs in my neighborhood and I found a live butterfly on the street. One of the butterfly's legs was broken and she couldn't fly. I picked her up and brought her to my home. When I showed her to my brother and my dad they were very happy to see this beautiful butterfly. My brother reminded me that butterflies do not have a very long life. I knew that I wanted to keep her safe and comfortable for as long as possible. I took her to my meditation room and prayed for her to complete her journey in the holy space of this room. This butterfly let me understand more fully how beautiful and valuable life is and that we should always find opportunities to provide a safe environment for other beings.

We Are Protected and Protector

In life sometimes we do not know whether we are on the right path and if we are living our life in harmony with our surroundings. We doubt ourselves and wonder if our actions are the best possible choices we could take at any given time. This was the question I pondered while walking my dogs in the neighborhood one day, when I came across a piece of tree bark that looked like an angel. The message and the confirmation I was looking for from the Universe were in this tree bark in the shape of an angel. I felt angels protecting me. I did not have to be concerned about my action and choices as long as I did the best I could do. A few days after I found this angel I received a confirmation from another friend that my action had positively influenced the life of a person that I had been concerned about. Through this connection I felt that we have angels' protection all around us and that the angel essence of our being changes our lives and the lives of others.

How LOVE Works

My assistant is from the Philippines. A few days after typhoon Haiyan hit his country, he told me that his community here wanted to have a garage sale and then send all proceeds from this garage sale to the Philippines. He asked me if I had anything to give them for their cause. He told me on Tuesday and the garage sale was Saturday of the same week. I decided to send an email to my friends inviting them to donate stuff they didn't need for the garage sale fund raiser that my assistant was setting up for the people in the Philippines. Also I went through my stuff and found a lot of items for him. The day after I sent the emails I received so many good items from everyone that my back yard and garage were full of clothes, books, furniture, light fixtures, frames, etc. It was an overflow of abundance and the grace of God was present in the goodness of everyone. My assistant and his community raised over $2,000.00 in that garage sale.

On Monday when he told me how much they had raised I felt so much joy and gratitude. I recognized an outstanding connection of community in this process. I remembered the following poem from Rumi that is about how LOVE works:

This piece of food cannot be eaten,
Nor this bit of wisdom found by looking,
There is a secret core in everyone,
Not even Gabriel can know by trying to know.

The Power Inside The Names of God

One day I was invited to a Christmas Holiday breakfast gathering with some friends. I decided to create a gift for everyone in this gathering using one Name of God for each person. My intention was that when everyone had a name, they would be connected to the energy of that name and would know that the power of that Name of God was protecting them. Each person picked one name at random. After each person shared about their past year and their New Year Resolutions; we noticed that the protection of the Name of God that each person had picked up was matched with their last year's journey and the next year's resolutions. It was so profound to see and feel how each Name of God protects us at any given time and gives us the security and connection we need to go through our life journey. The Name of God that I picked was "*The Watchful*". I felt a more powerful connection with God watching over me and providing everything that needs to unfold in my life. This was a great acknowledgement and it helped me to connect to the Divine Love even more profoundly.

Life Journey

In December 2013, I was on an airplane with my friends going to Mexico. From the airplane window I saw a cloud that was so beautiful! This cloud was like the side of the face of a child next to the side of the face of an old person. These two profiles were facing in the opposite direction from each other and were surrounded with other clouds. I saw my own life in this cloud and the process of my life journey. The face of the child was expressing the freshness and innocence that I came into this life with and the face of the old person was expressing my life journey, the achievement of my wisdom from the work of my life. The cloud on top of the child's head was darker than the cloud on top of the old person. My understanding from looking at this cloud was this: my life and being part of this existence came from God's Love for me, but I leave this life with clarity about the true meaning of the Love of God. To me this is the best confirmation I can receive from the Universe that I am on the right path and in harmony with what God has planned for my life.

Gratitude

A few years ago I was the student of a master and I went to his retreats every month. The retreats were on a very beautiful ranch outside the city. On this ranch there was a big circular area facing the mountains. We would gather there and our teacher would sit on the pedestal above us facing us and the mountain. One day all of us had to do service projects in silence and our service duties were chosen randomly by the staff. My service project was to clean the path that our teacher would walk to get to his spot and the area where he sat. I was very happy when they gave me this job. I cleaned the pathway and his space with a broom. Although I was supposed to be in silence I was so happy that I was singing to myself as I was cleaning the area. When our service projects were finished and we attended class with our teacher to share our experiences, one of the people in the retreat raised her hand and told our teacher that I had been singing when I was doing my service and she had really enjoyed the sound of my voice. My teacher asked me why I was singing? I said I was very happy with the work I was doing; I was cleaning the pathway for my teacher and I was honored that the Universe had chosen this job for me.

In December of 2013 I was invited by a friend to go to Mexico. She had a 90 year old husband and she couldn't take him on this trip without my help. I was honored to receive this invitation and to be of service for my friend and her wonderful husband. When we got to our hotel, which was a majestic 500 year old palace, the staff took me to my room and I was filled with tears of gratitude. The walkway to my room was like the path I had cleaned in my retreat service project several years earlier. The window in my room opened to an arena for horseback riding and it had a view of the mountain. When I sat on the chair in front of my window balcony I felt I was sitting on my teacher's pedestal. As a service project several years ago I had been cleaning such a place for a master and now as a service project I was honored to stay in a place like that because of my friend's invitation. My heart was filled with gratitude and the connection to the Love of my Beloved God.

Many years ago I had opened myself to knowing my Beloved God, and this experience was the result of my patience and the reward for my dedication. This experience was the fruit of years of hard work and a very deep connection to the spirit of service. Now I was in the place I had once cleaned for a teacher and my friends were now taking care of me, all expenses paid. I was awed by and grateful to the magic of service.

The Beauty of Life

On one of my trips I visited a majestic palace in Mexico. In this palace were several peacocks walking around the garden area every day. I really wanted to see one of them with open tail feathers in his glorious elegant pose. One day as I was walking to the restaurant I saw one of them in his cage with his feathers spread. He was so beautiful! I went to his cage and took a picture of him. He didn't close his tail when I got close, nor did he try to attack me. He was not afraid of me and it was as if he knew that I would not hurt him. He was expressing his beauty fully and I could enjoy him fully. Then it occurred to me that my wish had been fulfilled.

At that moment I wondered what was the significance of him inside the cage manifesting his beauty with his open tail? I felt he didn't open his tail when he was outside because a lot of people were around him out there and he wasn't feeling safe; but in his cage he felt safe and he showed his beauty. I wondered where do I open my wings and let my beauty show fully? It came to me that I feel safe to spread my wings when I feel the presence of God within me. Symbolically my surrender to God's Will is my cage. When I feel the Beloved protection I feel safe and willing to allow my wings open and show the beauty of my soul to the world.

God's Mercy

One day during my Mexico trip, my friends took me to another city one hour away from the place where we were staying. A taxi picked us up from our hotel and drove us there. The road was a very narrow one going through the mountains and I was sitting in front next to our driver. As I was looking everywhere and connecting to my surroundings I noticed a black dog dying on the side of the road with his eyes open and helpless. We couldn't stop to pick him up and I don't think that even if we could have stopped we would have done so. I was heartbroken when I saw that dog there and I knew I couldn't do anything for him. I was in tears for the rest our drive until we got to Taxco. I have two dogs and I love them very much, so seeing a dog dying on the side of the road alone was very painful. When we got to Taxco there was a beautiful church in the center of town. I went inside the church and prayed for that dog. I put some money in the donation box next to the statue of a Saint, and I asked the spirit of that Saint to hold the dog in his arms until he completed his journey. When we got back to our hotel I told my friend and showed her the picture of that Saint. She told me that this was St. Michael and that he represents the Mercy of God. Suddenly it was clear that my prayer had been answered and that that dog didn't die alone. Everyone needs a caring touch when they are transitioning. If I can't provide that caring touch I can ask for help and pray to God. This event grounded me in the value of life, the power of prayer and in holding loving space for the needy ones.

Unconditional Love

A few days before my first Rumi workshop when I was walking in nature and contemplating my Rumi workshop with the Universe I found a piece of wood. The shape of this wood was like that of a person kneeling down with a torch in her hand. The next Saturday I gave my first Rumi Workshop and it was amazing! Two of my old friends who have known me for a long time attended my workshop. These friends have known me since my darkest days and they have witnessed the evolution in my life. After the workshop had finished, one of them told me how happy she was to see me holding the torch of Unconditional Love. At that moment I was filled with gratitude for how well the Universe had answered my prayer and confirmed that I was on the right path.

Held by Divine Love

On one of my hikes I wanted to know how my relationship with God looked from God's point of view. This thought was at the center of my meditation hike on that day and I asked God to answer my question. As I was hiking I found a small stone in the shape of a heart. I was so happy, I thought the answer to my question was God telling me, *"I love you"*. As I continued my hike I found another stone and I picked up that one also. I couldn't recognize the shape of that stone but my intuition told me to hold on to it, that it had a message for me. When I got to the spot where I usually sit and meditate on the top of the mountain, I looked at both stones and experienced an Aha! moment. The second stone I had found looked like the palm of a hand and the first stone, shaped like a heart, fit inside the palm of the hand perfectly. God was telling me *"I am holding you in my palm"*. I was in tears when I received this message and overwhelmed with gratitude and humility that I am protected by God and Divine Love. I brought those stones home and placed them in my kitchen next to the sink so I can see them every day and be reminded that God is holding me in the palm of His Hand and I am protected by Divine Love.

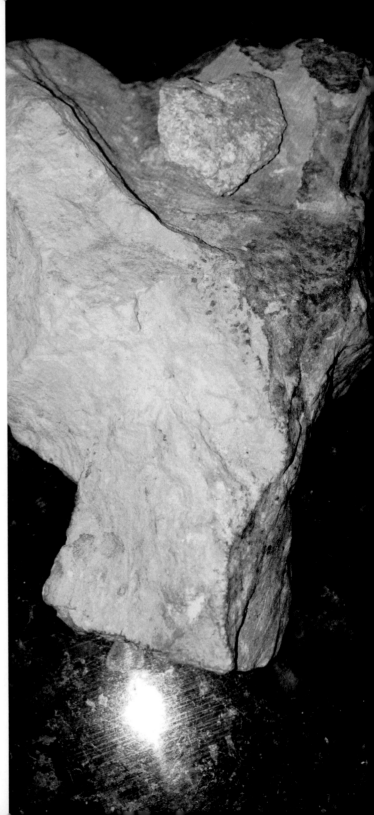

Connecting to Divine Love

A few days after one of my Consciousness, Health, and Healing (CHH) weekend class where we had been working on the 4th chakra, (which stands for *"The power of Divine Love"),* I was very emotional and somehow disconnected from the reality of this life. I really didn't know what was going on with me and why I felt that way. I asked God to help me, to guide me to the Light within my feeling and to ground me in the power of this Light. That day one of my vendors came to my office and we were talking about how we were going spend our Holiday. He started telling me a story about his 2 year old son. He said when he put his son to bed at night, the baby normally drank his milk bottle and went to sleep. On Christmas night his son got up from his bed, reached to the table next to his bed, picked up a cross and held it to his chest, and then he went to sleep. When his dad went to check on him he was so surprised to see him holding the cross. That cross had been on that table for over a year and his son had never been interested in it until that night. The dad took a picture of him holding the cross as he slept. When he showed me his son's picture, it occurred to me that this was the True Connection that my heart desired while I had been looking for this connection in my emotions.

This explained why I felt the way I had felt and the power working inside me. The picture of that child took me to my childhood and true connection with the unconditional love I received from my family. It was powerful enough to make me feel whole again and receive *"the Power of Divine Love".*

Beauty of Love in any Shape in Nature

On one of my walks with my dogs, I was admiring the beautiful roses in front of the various houses and was connecting to their soft look and beauty. I saw a piece of wood in the shape of a rose on the ground. I picked it up and looked at it. I had never seen anything like this before. A few steps after that I found another piece of wood shaped like a rose. I picked up the second rose-shaped piece of wood too. They both looked like roses but one was soft, delicate, and colorful, while the others were hard and dark. Then I saw the beauty of the roses in front of the houses in contrast to these wooden roses that I held in my hand. This experience opened me to the beauty of love that is in everything in Nature and everything on my life path. Beauty is part of everything in Nature and the Divine Being. If I accept this I can connect to the gifts they bring to my life and can connect more deeply to the ultimate Beauty of Love that is my Divine Being.

Grace of Gratitude

I had to smog check my car and I went to a mechanic's shop to get this job done. After my smog check was completed the service man came to me, shook my hand and thanked me for bringing the grace of prosperity to his life by bringing my business to him. I had never come across any mechanic who showed his appreciation and gratitude like he did. I was very grateful to experience that and very happy that I had taken my business to him and had received his appreciation. I left his shop with my heart full of the joy of gratitude that he had given me. When I was driving home I saw a homeless man with a sign in his hand asking for help. I gave him $5.00 and he was very happy; he told me he was going to Carl's Jr. to eat and he thanked me for my generosity. I felt that the homeless man had received from me the gratitude that I had received from the mechanic. At that moment, I connected to the energy of "*what goes around comes around*" and acknowledged that I like the connection of giving and receiving gratitude in my daily life. That power of gratitude was enough to make my day meaningful and to fill me with the joy of life.

Guided by The Divine Father

One day when I was walking with my dogs, I saw another dog like my dogs but much bigger. It was so nice to see them together being from the same breed but in different sizes. I became deeply aware that we are all the same breed because the breath of God is in all of us but in different shapes and forms. As we hold our dogs on their leashes, so too, we are held with Divine Love's invisible leash. Just as we protect our dogs, Divine Love is protecting us. If I practice remembering that I am held by Divine Love's invisible leash, then I can experience more joy and less fear in my life. When it is not safe, Divine Love pulls back on my leash and protects me from those that look like me, but whose intentions could harm my wellbeing. It is the same way with any dog owner who protects their pet from an aggressive dog.

Spiritual Teacher

I am a life student of Rumi and I honor Shams, Rumi's teacher. Shams was an old man, deeply connected to Divine Love, who lived his life with the Love of God. Rumi noticed this man and his Divine qualities. He followed his path and became the enlightened person we know. Shams's wisdom was not known to the common people but Rumi noticed the Light and Wisdom in him and became his student.

Danny is the representation of Shams in my life and the person who saw the beauty of my soul when I couldn't see it at all. He guided me to connect to the Light of my soul. Any time I felt lost and I couldn't find my way past obstacles in day to day life, I either could go to him or I could ask myself how Danny would handle this matter. Danny is very intelligent and he has a kind heart. His manner is pure, his being is free of any expectation, and his connection to Divine Love is like the bright sun. I saw that his Light was not visible to everyone but no one could deny his presence.

Danny is my Shams, he is the person who saw the majesty of my soul when no one, not even myself, could see it, and he walked me through the dark night of my life. He is my first spiritual teacher and his presence guides me in dealing with the unexpected challenges that come into my life.

Surrender to What Is

These days my mind is very preoccupied and I feel I have more on my plate than I can handle. With my losing a big account and being unfairly accused of something that I need to clear up with my client, I know I have to shift gears and raise my consciousness in order to find the way to handle my life. One day when I was walking in my neighborhood I saw a Buddha statue in the front yard of a house. The calmness, serenity, and beauty of this space enhanced the whole street and everyone passing by was drawn to it. This Buddha statue was in the place that gets cold during the night, exposed to bright sun, noise, dust, rain, and other elements of nature, still it was so calm and peaceful that it was affecting its surroundings. That front yard raised my consciousness and opened me to the compassion and courage I needed to be with myself in the midst of the big waves going on in my life.

Enhance The Beauty

During one period of my life I really needed to connect to the beauty and joy that were going on in my life. I was under a lot of pressure and I felt my life was out of balance. I noticed that I had to make an effort to bring joy and beauty into my daily life. In the midst of what I was going through, a friend of mine was having a birthday. She was turning 60 and her daughter was giving a big party for her. I went to buy her a gift. In the parking lot I saw a Mini Cooper and the owner had put eyelashes on the headlights of her car. My first reaction was to laugh, then connect to the creativity of the car's owner, and the joy she presented in her car to others. Also, I noticed how the appearance of this car was changed by a minor touch that made it more beautiful. I asked myself, how can I enhance my life? How can I add a small touch to what is going on in my life now? And how can I bring more humor to the situation and express the true beauty of who I am and the joy I feel in my heart? Seeing the eye lashes of this Mini Cooper created the shift I needed to release the pressure I had been feeling. Then I could step up to creative ways of dealing with the tasks in my life.

Hold On to Balance

A few years ago I went to Ethiopia with one of my spiritual teachers. We visited a church that had been carved from one piece of stone; the cross of that church was called the *"Balance Cross"*. I bought several Balance Cross charms and when I came back I gave them as gifts to everyone. A few months later I realized I hadn't kept one for myself. Then later I went to Minnesota to visit my parents, and my mother's nurse gave me a Balance Cross necklace. I was so very happy to receive it and since that time I have always worn it. This charm has kept me grounded and always connects me to the balance I want in my life. These days this charm hanging around my neck is protecting my heart from the storms I feel in my life, and it gives me strength to stay in balance. The Divine Love and Grace in that church built from solid stone are in this necklace and they are helping me to stay grounded. This necklace helps me do whatever is necessary to manifest the energy of the *"Balance Cross"*, the Voice of God and God's Beauty. I was never connected to this charm before the way I am now as I receive its protection.

Rooted to The Center of Earth and Divine Love

A few days ago while I was walking with my dogs, I was preoccupied with my thoughts and the problems I was having with a client, the account that I had lost, and their false accusation. I was asking God to give me a sign and let me see the good that is happening in this situation. I passed by a home and in the front yard there was a strong tall old tree with no leaves. Although it looked dead, actually it was alive. Beautiful even with no leaves on it and it gives service to the owners. I saw two swings hanging from a tree branch and some nice chairs and a table in the front yard. This tree looked nice in their yard and it brought joy to their children.

I tried to compare what I was going through with this tree. I have strong roots like this tree. It occurred to me that this was the answer I was looking for. It doesn't matter what is happening on the surface, I still have a lot of opportunities to do my best and to provide service to everyone who crosses my path. I stand for simplicity, dignity, service, and beauty. These are the qualities I want to be present in my life and to offer to everyone involved in it just like this tree does. So why should I worry about the people who don't see the qualities of my being in my work? I realized that what I am going through is not that bad and, actually, it is very nice!

The people causing me this agony are like beggars looking for shelter to get by for one night. They think they have to get ahead and they can't connect to the simple elements of integrity, respect and honesty. They do not understand the true meaning of working together and helping each other. They miss the goodness of life which mutual respect brings to each other. Now I have compassion for my client and I can find the strength to deal with my situation with grace and the understanding of Unconditional Divine Love.

In my workshop on Consciousness, Health, and Healing (CHH) we were working with the 6th chakra (that represents the energy of *"Wisdom and Seeing Clearly and Compassionately"*) and I had a big breakthrough. I noticed that my inner child was scared and afraid of being alone. I remembered that the first time I felt this way was when I was 3 years old. It was 11:00 pm at night when someone came to our home and gave my family the news that my aunt and her children had died in an earthquake in Iran. My parents and grandparents were so sad after that news that they couldn't give me the attention I needed as a 3 year old child. I was left alone for a long time and had no one to love me for several months. That was the first time I experienced detachment and the fear of not being loved. In that CHH weekend I faced my scared and angry child for the first time. She did not trust me and I felt paralyzed. I really didn't know how to show her my love and earn her trust. I felt the pain and sadness in my heart. I wanted to heal the small child inside of me. Then I realized my 3 year old inner child's experience was the seed of who I am today. As an adult I have used that energy to look for Unconditional Love that would never leave me, so I would always feel safe. That pain from my childhood eventually drove me to look for the Love of God and led me to become a wise woman. However, it was clear to me that although I am now a wise woman, I still did not know how to deal with this inner angry, hurt child.

I noticed for the first time in a very long time that I had been wanting to hold myself often. My inner child needed my unconditional love, and now my focus was to give her love, attention, and help her to heal from her painful past experience. These days I was very emotional and I cried a lot. Often I held myself like someone holding a child, putting my right arm to my left shoulder and my left arm around my stomach. A few days after this awareness, while walking in my neighborhood, I saw a mother and child sitting outside their front door on the ground, eating cereal. I asked if I could take a picture of them and she gave me permission. Looking at the connection they had with each other gave me hope, and I had the intention to create the same loving connection for myself and my inner child. This event helped me to recognize the love that I had been missing in my life. When my inner child is healed, she will feel secure enough to be around me; and she can become a healthy child full of vitality and we can have a lot of fun together.

The next day I bought myself a doll to represent my inner child. I named her "Gi Joon" which means "Sweet Dear Little Getty". During the first week of our reconnection, my doll and I were always together. We walked, ate, slept, and even went to work with each other. Both of us were healing with this reunion; "Gi Joon" is such a joyful child and she trusts me as her caregiver and her companion now. At last both of us are grateful for this reunion and the unconditional love between us.

Rooted in Mother Nature
Facing Divine Love

I have a lot on my mind: healing my inner child, losing two more clients, and dealing with transferring their accounts to new management companies takes a lot out of me. In the past I would hike every morning and I have not done that for quite a long time. I decided to go back to Mother Nature alone, without my dogs, and to connect to her energy again. On my hike I asked Mother Nature to heal me and to give me a sign that she was working on my healing. On my way down in the distance I saw a dry plant that was not on the main path I hike. This plant looked different. I changed my path to look at it more closely. When I got close, the plant did not look like anything I had ever seen before. It looked like a sun rooted to earth with two branches on each side rising to the sky. This plant was facing east, from where the sun rises. I felt this plant was telling me who I am. I am the representation of the sun on the earth, grounded in my love for God, and holding my arms up asking for direction and guidance from the Beloved. That plant off of the main trail was the sign from God showing me His support. In that moment it was clear to me in order to experience such a magnificent beauty, it is necessary to get off the main path.

Life Is Full of Life

On one of my daily walks with my dogs I had a question. I wanted to know how to manage my energy, stay connected to Divine Love, and trust the process. I came across a home in my neighborhood that I had not noticed before. This home looked like the houses in the desert, with a lot of cactus and a very simple appearance. In the front yard, there was a well and around it was a beautiful grape vine.

My emotions are like this home in the dessert, the well is the symbol of my faith in Divine Love, the grape vine around the well represent the essence of life within me. I saw that it is very hard for me to vision the essence of life in the midst of my emotions.

I had an epiphany in that moment. Now, I know what I needed to do. I had to direct my attention to Divine Love so I could connect to the essence of life in the midst of my emotions. This simple vision gave me courage and helped me to trust the process I was going through.

The Way God Is with Me

March 21st is the Iranian New Year and this celebration is very holy for me. I normally set a table for ceremony and have a powerful ritual with my family and I give meaningful gifts to everyone. This year I was so preoccupied with my life that I didn't have the time or the energy to do any of these things and I was not feeling complete with the New Year. I asked God to guide me: how can I connect to this energy and deliver the message of the New Beginning? The next day a friend called and invited me to a New Year gathering in her home. The day before the New Year gathering a message came to me. The message was to make coasters with a Name of God on each one and to give them as gifts to everyone at the gathering. That night I made 36 coasters to take with me to our New Year gathering. Each person had to make a meaningful wish about what they wanted to manifest in their life in the coming year. The Name of God that they picked would be the way in which God would help them accomplish their wish. When I finished making these coasters I took a moment for myself. I prayed and I picked up a coaster. The message for me was *"The Guide"*. I understood that God guides me and my job is to follow Him. I put this coaster on my office desk to stay connected while I am working and giving my service to others. This coaster is my reminder for the year to trust the energy of this God Name to guide me in every step I take.

The

Guide

Being in Gratitude

A day after I made the coasters I was driving to my friend's place for our New Year gathering. I was thinking what my job this year is based on the message I had received on my coaster. Suddenly I saw that there was a car in front of me on the highway with the license plate *"THKUGOD"*. I couldn't believe my eyes! It was like a weight lifted off my shoulders. God is in the midst of everything that is happening and I have to stay in gratitude this year no matter what life presents me.

At this time in my CHH class I was working on the 6th chakra (which has the energy of *"Wisdom and Seeing Clearly and Compassionately"*). That car's license plate guided me to focus on my communication with God, to trust the process, and to be thankful for every lesson. I received my confirmation that God knows what is going on in my life and my job is to follow God's guidance with gratitude in my heart.

Reborn

Last year I bought a Dahlia bush and planted it in my back yard but it seemed to die right away. I never saw any flowers blooming on it. In the winter I cut off all the branches and left the roots in the ground. In the spring a few days after I had started hiking again and connecting to Mother Nature, I saw the first flowers on that plant. The flowers were so beautiful and so alive!!! The mixed colors of red and white reflected the union of the blood in my body as the essence of my life with the Light of God as the essence of my soul mixed together in my being. This beautiful flower showed me that when I feel disconnected, it is as if my branches are dead, but in time my soul helps me to find my connection again, and I am reborn with a higher consciousness. It occurred to me that the winter of my disconnection had passed and now my body, mind, and soul were coming forth to show their beautiful essence. This flower illustrates the gifts of the different seasons in my being, the connection to the life of each season, and how to rise up to the direct connection which is True Faith.

Dancing with The Flow

During a break in my CHH class, working with the 7th chakra, (which has the energy of *"Living in the Precious Presence"),* I went for a walk in the neighborhood. I saw a sign on a tree in front of a home. The wording on the sign was *"What if The Hokey Pokey is Really What It's All About?".* I didn't know the meaning of Hokey Pokey but I felt I had to take a picture of that sign and let the true meaning reveal itself to me in due time. A few days after our weekend class I asked a friend what was the meaning of Hokey Pokey, and she told me that it is a kind of dance and she described that dance to me. I knew that this dance represents the relationship of Lover and Beloved. I asked myself how am I dancing with my Beloved? My life is not in order because I am out of practice with my steps. I needed to start practicing my dance with the Beloved again. In the past I took time to spend with Mother Nature every morning and I opened my mind to Her Voice. I had not done that for a long time and our connection had suffered. It came to me that I need to get back to this practice and start my hikes again. Now after two weeks of waking up before dawn, hiking, and communing with Mother Nature I am dancing with more harmony and I am experiencing more peace and serenity in my life.

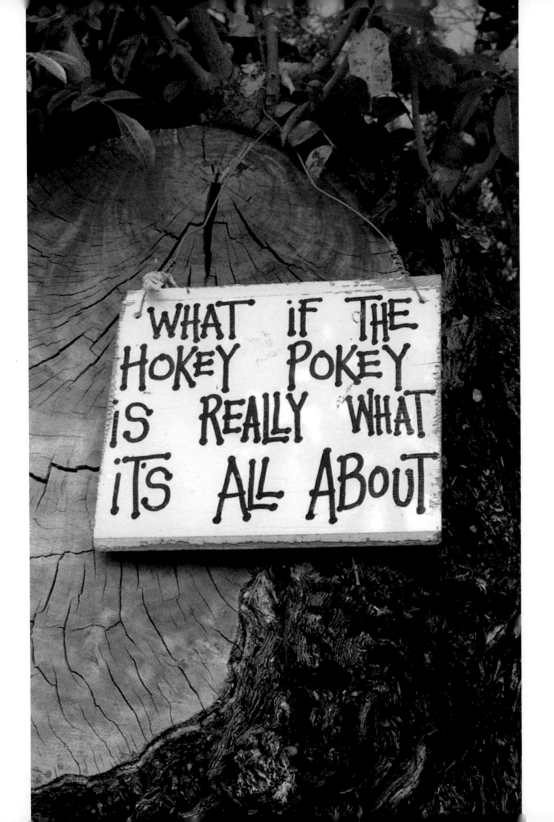

Souls Never Die and Are Always with Us

I lost one of my Rumi classmates; she was a very nice, caring student who was dedicated to our teacher and to Rumi teaching. None of us knew she was sick and her death was a surprise to all of us. Her family arranged a service for her in her home and we went there to give them our support. On that day I asked her spirit to let me know if she had any messages for her family. In my meditation I felt that she was in a very good place and she was looking after her family.

When I arrived at her home all our friends were there. Her spirit had brought all of us together again, sharing our love with her spirit and with each other. Her daughter took us to her back yard and showed us her garden. She had a green thumb and her yard was a wonderful space. As we walked around her yard admiring everything she had planted, I turned my face to the sky and saw a cloud in the shape of an angel. I knew it was her spirit looking down on us but I didn't want to say that to the other people. I told everyone to look at that cloud and one of the friends said it looked like an angel; then I said it was her spirit looking after her home and her family. We went around to the side of her home to look at trees she had planted and we returned to the back yard in less than five minutes. The cloud was gone. Then I knew for sure that the cloud was her spirit. Her spirit's love opened us to deeper listening in silence. The Spirit Voice through that cloud helped my healing from losing a friend and it gave comfort to her family knowing she was looking after them.

After that, her daughter and grandchildren were relieved. This was the confirmation they needed to know that their mother was at peace and looking after them.

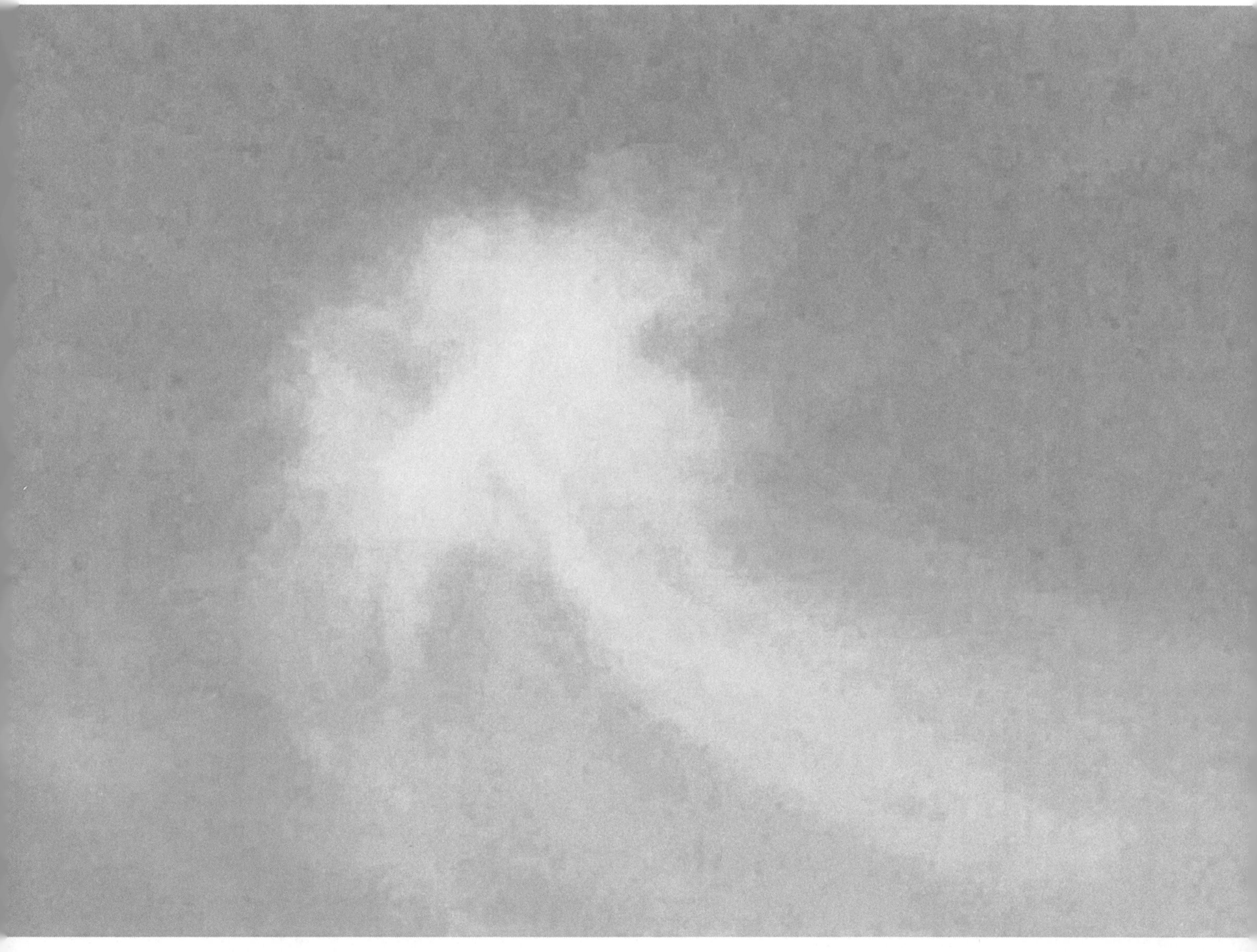

New Life

A month after I had seen that dry plant mentioned in the story *"My Being Is Rooted in Mother Nature and Facing Divine Love"*, I was hiking on the same mountain again. Although I hiked every day, that day I decided to take the path where I had found that dry plant. I was very happy that I had come back to the mountain again and was starting my day with my Mother Nature connection. Then on the same path, I found a rock in the shape of a heart. This rock was so beautiful! It was like a heart-shaped bowl that fit perfectly in my hand.

This Rock was the symbol of my receiving Mother Nature energy and my connecting to my authentic self. I was filled with gratitude and my heart was oozing out joy at my reconnection. I truly love this rock because it is the symbol of my New Life with my Beloved and my feeling it deeply.

The Potential of Life

One day I was very tired and was needing a relaxing time with someone. I called a friend of mine to see if she was willing to have dinner. She was available and we went to dinner and a movie afterwards. On the way to the movie she pointed out an empty area on the side of the street. There was no plant in that area but the soil was wet and in the shape of a heart. It was so interesting to see that space. It became clear to me that before having dinner with my friend I was like this empty space; I had love and life but not fully present at that time. I was like this area with soil in the shape of a heart but no plant in that wet soil. After dinner and the movie I was alive again. I felt that through my friend, God's helping hand had manifested what I needed to rejuvenate myself. This heart reminded me while I was in one of the low points of my life that the Love of God and the Breath of Life were in the midst of helping me to rise up and rejuvenate my life essence.

Creativity of My Being

A few days ago I was occupied with my thoughts. I had lost a few accounts in the past few months and was asking God to guide me. How can I be more creative and generate more income to protect my family, business and the people working for me? I was driving and I saw a homeless person on the corner of the street. His appearance attracted everyone's attention. He used his imagination; everything about him was artistic. Looking at him delighted me because, although he was asking for help, he was using his creativity to give something to others by making himself interesting to the people passing that corner. He gave me the courage to look inside myself at my creativity and find an interesting way to present them. In that moment it dawned on me that I had the opportunity to establish a new business that could create more income and take advantage of my abilities. The next day I registered the name for my new business, got all the banking and advertising done, and started marketing for new clients. That homeless man was the messenger for my new horizon. Now, when I look at his picture I do not see a homeless man, I see a creative person who uses his gifts to better his life and the lives of others. This event was a magnificent opening for me and I hope that with the money I gave him I was blessing his life.

Happiness Is Who I Am

I really do not know if it is just me or if everyone goes through periods when they wonder if they are doing everything they can for the people they care about. My brother and his wellbeing are very important to me and I would like to do everything I can to help him establish his business. I was hiking early one morning and this thought was occupying my mind. I asked Mother Nature to assist me with how to accomplish this task and to guide me to the steps I should take. As I was driving back home from my hike, the license plate on the car ahead of me was *"BE HAPY"*. When I saw that I laughed. I saw that my worry and concerns were blocking me from doing the best I could do for him and for myself. This license plate reminded me that when I have the right question it takes only a few seconds to get my answer and to see the Divine Guidance that focuses me in the right direction. The message on that license plate gave me the courage to let go and let God protect me, and to be happy for everything I can do without attachment to the outcome.

53

Whirling Dance with The Divine

A friend of mine from CHH took some pictures of me and I truly love the photos he took. The pictures show the essence of who I am and my Oneness with the Beloved. He drove me downtown where I could dance with my whirling clothes. While I was whirling I was detached from my surroundings and I was connected to that present moment. This picture shows me how the energy of the 7th chakra (which has the energy of *"Living in the Precious Presence"*) connects everything as I open myself and I am willing to receive it. This picture, to me, is the Ultimate Intimacy Dance of Lover with Beloved. Also it shows me how life can be when my body is grounded to the earth and my wings are open to the Love of the Universe.

The True Joy of Life

I love another picture that a friend took of me. In this picture I can see the true joy of my being. I noticed that so often in the past I was so busy trying to do the right thing that I forgot to enjoy the happiness within the process. This picture shows me how my life can be joyful and how precious these moments are. I laminated this picture and put it in my shower so I can see who I am first thing in the morning and can then be this Joyful person throughout the day.

Looking at my picture is very healing and it allows me to connect to more of the joy, laughter, and humor that I want in my life.

Divine Voice

A day after my CHH weekend class connecting to the 8ᵗʰ Chakra, (which has the energy of *"The Universal Spiritual Heart"),* I was hiking and thinking about the teaching of this weekend and how I could connect to the energy of the 8ᵗʰ Chakra. I was humbly asking God *"Show me who I am that I can show who you are."*

When I came home and opened my Rumi book I found my answer in this poem. This was the message I needed to truly experience what the mystics referred to as *"being a Man of God":* The Consciousness of Universal Spiritual Heart.

A lover has four streams inside,
Of water, wine, honey, and milk.
Find those in yourself and pay no attention
To what so-and-so says about such-and-such.
The rose does not care
If someone calls it a throne, or a jasmine.
Ordinary eyes categorize human beings.
That one is Zoroastrian. This one a Muslim.
Walk instead with the other vision given you,
Your first eyes. Bow to the essence
In a human being. Do not be content
With judging people good and bad.
The great blessing is that Shams
Has poured a strength into the ground
That lets us wait and trust the waiting.

The Blessing

In life the blessing of all people who touch our heart is always with us.

It doesn't matter if we can remember it or not,

It doesn't matter if we can feel it or not,

It doesn't matter if we believe in it or not,

It doesn't matter if they know their blessing helps us,

Protects us, or even is a shelter for us.

Their blessing is the basic tool that eventually takes us to the ultimate connection with the Beloved and to experience Ecstasy.

At that moment, we experience another being who takes the fear away and allows us to see everything and everyone in a different light.

Our judgmental mind will shut off when that happens and we are with the Creator on the Ocean of Unconditional Love.

A great opening in our hearts will happen for the rest of our natural life when the blessing of all those people who touched us is recognized and understood.

This threshold makes us connected and gives us the power of belonging.

With this understanding we transcend to somewhere unknown until that moment and then we recognize the joy of knowing that place from a long, long time ago.

In mysticism they call that place the Eternal Home of the Man of God.

Anyone who achieves this state of mind feels the ultimate safe, beautiful, comfortable, and joyful bliss.

With that state of mind we grasp the language of the Universe and the ability to communicate with that language to anything and anyone who crosses our life path.

All these elements combined allow any human being the satisfaction of the hardship of the journey to the unknown.

Still, it all began with a blessing.

Getty Azod

About Getty

Getty Azod is graduate of the Spiritual Psychology and Consciousness, Health, and Healing programs from the University of Santa Monica. She has studied Kabala Jewish Mysticism under Rabbi Goldberg, Eastern and Western Philosophy with Dr. Shahparaki, and Rumi teaching from the book of Masnavi with Dr. Parviz Sohabi. Her Rumi classes and workshops have been well received throughout the greater Los Angeles area. Her life purpose is to awaken her divine potential and her consciousness through cosmic connection.

"Communication Beyond Words" is a partial memoir of Getty's connection to the Divine and the inspirational messages she received through her connection.

www.daytodaybliss.com

Reading Line

Learn how your innermost thoughts and the details of your daily life can help you understand the simplicity of how God wants your life to be, and then, to be grateful for everything, good or bad, that comes into your life because everything in life has a purpose.

This book can open your eyes to the symbolic language of the universe and give deeper meaning to your daily life experiences.

The universe talks to us through signs and we need to learn this sign language. This book is full of examples of how even the smallest thing may have a message for us.

Selected Quotes

Coleman Barks, quotes from book *"A Year with Rumi"*, *"Daily Readings"* for stories *"The Journey"*, *"How LOVE Works"* and *"Divine Voice"*

John O'Neil, the creator of falcon picture for story *"Connecting to The Power of Spirit"*

Eric Weiss, the creator of two pictures for stories *"Whirling Dance with The Divine"* and *"The True Joy of Life"*

Printed in the United States
By Bookmasters